The Ghetto of Eden

Jasmin Oya

Copyright © 2012 Author Name
All rights reserved.
ISBN:1523822910
ISBN-13:9781523822911

In Loving Memory of Clifford Johnson, Jeffrey Reese and Clifford Waiters.

DEDICATION

In December 2013, I began to write my first book of poetry. I initially began by collecting all of my favorites and putting them together to make itself sort of presentable, to say the very least. I had no idea the journey that this writing experience would take me on. I've found myself along the way. This book is dedicated to the many experiences that Yahushua has granted me while incorporating the neighborhoods and villages that have raised me. This book would be impossible if it weren't for the constant love and push I received from those who loved me enough to tell me about myself. The experiences that I've endured over the last three years have all been collected and placed in this book as a reminder to myself and as a love poem to you.

CONTENTS

1 The Beginning of Man   6

2 The Fall of Man   71

The Beginning of Man

"Now the Lord God had planted a garden in the east, in Eden; and there he put the man he had formed." (Gen. 2:8)

1
GENE.

There is no love like the one that created it.

In the beginning, God forgot what He was doing.
He was five years old and drunk with his youth
and you.
    He was silly everyday and had fun all the while.
He was spinning out of control and He was control.
    and He looked back at His mess.
He called it good.
    and what a world He created.
He cried on the seventh day.
    for you do that when you see beauty.
He cried yesterday.
    for you do that when you see ugly.
He hasn't stopped yet.

Two Hearts Deep ⭐

The day you find love
> is probably the hardest day of your life,

or it's a Monday.

A rainy one.

I mean,
> no one really hugs you on this day.

There's nothing that special about it.

You wake up, do the things you're supposed to in order to stay alive
> and look presentable as to not embarrass the people

that already agreed to love you.

Then, you continue your day.

You may trip in public while listening to that one song that makes you feel good about yourself
> but then you don't feel good about yourself because you just tripped in public.

Life is like one big party and everyone got the invitation
> but you

and you're standing outside the big party waiting for everyone to come outside and leave because misery loves
> Company.

But, you don't like that too much, do you?

Company:

Over five people breathing the same air as you,

telling better jokes

or worse ones

but you fake laugh because some one taught you how.

But, you can't remember who.

Company.

You hate it and you can't imagine marriage, right? You can't imagine wanting someone every second of the day. You think that's unattractive. You think that about yourself sometimes. You think no one would want to be around you for so damn long.

You are overflowing with flaws and you do a pretty decent job of making sure everyone sees them.

You want to make sure no one overstays their welcome.

You think you do all the time.

And then you meet them.

They make you want to be lonelier than you were yesterday.

You've found someone to be lonely with.

You can unbuckle your pants and let your stomach creep over your waist. Your hair is a little less kept and you have a mouth spilling of morning breath.

You forget they are there sometimes because you are being your alone self.

You can feel their company. You love their company.

You bask in the thang.

You love all the lives inside them.

And you are always flying a little above everyone else.

The world is clearer from up here,

The air is just fine up here.

And suddenly, Mondays aren't so bad.

Adam

The day I learned her body to be mine
I searched our skins for sense.
I placed my hands in hers and we were prayer.
We gave earth a name.
We gave sound a language.
We dipped our tongues in a river of dialect and decorated
our conversation with it.
The sea was an endless yawn,
waters stretching their arms to hug the wind
brushing waves licking the edge.
The sky blushing
a cherry hue,
flirting with the day.
We bathed in her rivers
recognized Him in every detail.
The small light cradling our bronze reflection smiling back
at us.
We never named the magic.
We danced it and we couldn't imagine a world less.
Birth me something anew in that smile,   I rest in.
I found a home that I cannot let go of.
We are a joy that someone's preying to put in their bones.

The Ghetto of Eden

There is a laugh that drips from your lips
shadowing the ground
flowing behind you.
May this skin be mine no longer.
She has touched me and turned my body into a gold key.
Black and bright.
unlocking every door in her,
giving the anatomy a name.
I named your body after her in every language,
in every tongue.
Look at the light peeking through the cracks,

like a small girl standing in her parent's doorway afraid of the

storm

outside.

Come.
Celebrate her with me.
Worship Him with me.
For they have both given my bones a reason.
Sometimes, when I listen closely
I
hear the sky falling

or she's calling my name.
Have you ever not known
whether to run
or to answer.

The Negro

There is a Negro that knows nothing of his skin. He knows that it itches and when he scratches, it turns to ash. He knows that blood pours from it when it opens and it burns. He believes that it hurts even when no harm is being done to it. He doesn't believe that he's related to it for we are all just people, aren't we? Humanity is a race and this skin was made a reminder against him. A betrayal of his body. So, we are all just human and skin doesn't matter. He says this because he is not friends with his skin. His skin is his enemy that he takes long walks with. His skin is his enemy that he sweats with. His skin is his enemy that catches his tears when they come and holds them back when he'd rather them not. His skin is his enemy that he bathes and moisturizes. His skin is his enemy that he bandages when it is wounded. His skin is his enemy that his mother kissed when outside bruised it. His skin is his enemy that he cannot keep his hands off of. He finds no joy in this skin or anyone else's skin that looks like his. He knows he hates it. He wants everyone to stop noticing it. He wants everyone to stop seeing it. Stop talking about it. Stop shooting it. Stop policing it. Stop kissing it. Stop picking at it. He doesn't know if this is him protecting it or if it is him hiding it. He knows that a white family just moved in down the block. He knows that the black family moved out. He knows that Uncle Lapp's Soul Food spot has closed and a man who wears a suit and has blue eyes that only sees green has bought it. He knows they are gutting it out. They are loud about it. They sing it to him every night. He knows they are raising taxes and his friends are drowning, kissing his skin goodbye with their lives in their palms.

Grandma's Tongue

I know there's a word for the blood in here.
That a phrase lives on some other tongue, either buried or breathing
and I was taken away from her.
On the backs of promise and dream,
I know there's a sentence for this moment.
There's a love for this loss.
An embrace for this lonely.
They are in some land looking for me
as I stand here
searching for that word
the English language
never thought to define or speak.
They never made enough room for my loss
or my stolen.
The word is wrapped around some other tongue dancing
back and forth in conversation and in song.
In bickering and goodbye.
In love and dream.
I am desperately scraping my knees trying to get to it.
We've been craving this holy ground
this forsaken language.

yet we settle for sadness.

we drown the search in drunk.

We kiss it in sex.

We love it in marriage.

We dance it in electric.

We cook it in grease.

We praise it in church.

We rub it in scalp.

We sing it in jazz.

We rap it in rhyme.

We go on and on...

Gift

I want to put my body in a gentle man's arms.
        I want to give me to him.
        I want him to pray to someone in the sky
            And say thank you for it.

The Prayer

I believe in God like I believe in my mother's palms.

    I believe in Him like I believe in my mother's mouth and knees.

Her tongue and every hallelujah that
    yawned with it.

I see Him in her posture.

    I've been trying to mirror it since young
since young,
        I've been trying to reflect her old.

All the prayers that have seen more days than me.

    The ones answered and the ones that haven't/won't/will

    For I am no one without them.
    For I am one with them.
    For I breathe because they did.

    I believe in God like I believe in tomorrow.

    I believe in Him like I believe in today.

    How exhausting they both can be
        smelling of morning breath,
prayer and gospel.

These days aren't easy, most of them are lies about what's really hurting,

> *what lies beneath,*
> *who we are when*
> *the room is empty.*
> *when they've all gone home.*

> *the party is over.*   *the*
> *decorations are worn.*
> *the night is fast asleep,*
> *you're left wondering,*
> *who turned off all the music.*
> *where have all the people gone.*
> *who stopped dancing first.*

Prayers don't have room for the pride.

Put that to the side.

Gather yourself away from all the noise.

I'm learning to stop mourning the morning.

Find solace in the silence.

To stop fitting God into the nearest human body.

Believe in what I have yet to see.

BLACK BOY CHRONICLE

For the boy I shared my crayons with who colored the sidewalk red last night.

them black boys be bleeding.
black boy bleed black
until
black boy becomes bones
black boy bones
big boned baddies.
black boy bag bitches
black boy has no daddy.
black boy blows blunt.
black be bruised by black boy's bullets.
black boys be bullets…
bullets bleed black boys
black boys become just body.
black boy has baby.
black boy still has no daddy.
black boy has baby.
black boy still has no daddy.
black boy runs.
with the feet of a slave.
black boy runs.

leave a bitch when she's late.

black boy runs.

that baby is just another bullet anyway.

black boy runs.

black bitches scared of me anyway.

black boy runs…

find the nearest jail cell.

black man runs…

heaven is more expensive than hell.

black him runs.

the lies my dreams tell.

black hymn runs.

the truths my nightmares sing.

Bloody Reality

The only thing that can be raised that's brown
in this country is the sun.
My fear of having one is that there will be a morning
he won't wake up in.
And that morning....
that morning keeps me up at night.

Marvin's Room

The first time that I saw my father cry was when we were on our way home from North Carolina and we were driving through Virginia. The skies were blue and white pillows I couldn't tear my eyes from. My father's heavy arm wrapped itself around my shoulder with his other hand tapping away on the steering wheel. Marvin Gaye's "What's Goin' On" began to blast through the speaker. My father turned the volume down to tell me about his superhero. My father. Who would one day leave me like his father left him. My father. Who I'm still searching for in the things we once found sacred. My father. A blurry memory. My father. Felt safe enough to go to the place Marvin's music takes him right there in front of his daughter. I remember watching him tell me how Marvin Gaye was killed by his own father. After a while, he wasn't talking to me anymore. He was talking to the music. He was talking to the song. He was opening the door that so many black men hid behind. He was showing me them. Cowered into small nothings. He was letting me see the tears. He was letting me see the healing and all the wounds. He was open. I wasn't there anymore. It was just him and Marvin. Talking. Man to man. Saying, "I miss you, brother" in the most masculine way a man doesn't know how.

Wedding Night

The night will come

where the angels will request a leave from heaven.

The moon will come

bringing a galaxy as a host.

They will gather at our window.

They will be our only light.

I'll trace your back

with the same hands I used to pray

for you with.

Inscribing circles on your spine.

What a canvas you are,

What art we will make,

What hallelujah will come

when we do,

from the most deserted

alley in our guts

the most vacant parts of us alive and singing.

We will praise the body

and every flaw on it

turning every scar

this world has

left on us

into an open hymnal

I will sing you.

Make a sanctuary out of your chest.

This will be worship.

There will be no more waiting, my love.

We will be naked and miles from ashamed.

Letting the floor wear our clothes.

The only parts of us

that will be covered will be the skin under our ring

fingers

digging into flesh

until you live under my nails.

until I never pluck you out.

until the world beneath us

swings

back and forth like

wedding bells.

Like their tune,

we will collide.

we will break.

You'll make me whole again.

All in one night,

in just a series of breath and scar.

I will kiss the shadows behind your ears

Let there be light.

I will hover over you

Like the sky does the ocean. .

Our breaths will be

The atmosphere

in between.

Let there be wind

make a garden

out of my womb

Let us never

move from here.

Let time catch its breath.

Someone, tell the dawn I said hello.

Tell morning I couldn't make it

Send the sun my love.

Kiss the dew for me.

Surely, I have missed them all for my world.

And if love were a texture, it would be your skin.

Find me where the skin meets.

At some point, one realizes that they've become their oppressor. All the things they've ran from has consumed them. They're becoming the parents they didn't like and they are spouting the same words that someone used on them to silence the shine. Their tongue alone is making it difficult for someone else to breathe and to enjoy having to do so every day. They sound too much like the voices they've tried to escape or were so afraid, they stayed longer than they lived.

When you are speaking and you hear your oppressor louder than yourself, change your wishes. Make them simpler. Ask for a smoother tongue. One that doesn't leave lashes.

February 15th

1:43 A.M.

The night shrunk itself until it became our shadow.

We now have time

following us and

not us following time.

This is beautiful.

But we don't say it.

Yet

We know how to show it

To draw it.

You,

tracing your fingers up

and down my spine

like a car leaving tracks on a dirt road

until it's the only home

it has ever known.

Your sweaty palms are

the only home my

heart's ever known.

Look how crooked it is...

look how crooked we are

I am.

you see it

don't you?

the ugly flaws that won't leave.

when I said bare with me

I was asking for you to put

your naked on my skin.

Your cheek to my bone.

Your mouth to swallow my lips

whole until I am.

Again.

Lose the clothes.

Wear my body.

Hold my hands so tight

we'll bury fireworks

between them

that may we let go

It'll look like we have just been

Crucified.

Engrave your sweat into me.

Stain me with you.

Love the hell out of me you devil.

Love the heaven in me, you angel.

February 15th

2:07 A.M.

The Artists,

We know how to take your name and make you think that it only belongs on our tongue and that any other place is blasphemous. Our love is some kind of religious. We, writers, know how to love with our pens and write with our hearts. The most beautiful words living in us find the paper before they find the lover. And I am so lost. I am so lost in deciding what part of myself to give to the world and what to give you.

Her: Thoughts

My mother told me that when you fall in love with a man, he will fill you with himself if you are empty. She said that if there is nothing in you, he would plant himself in you. That's just fine. For you are made from a man so, in a way, you are reuniting with yourself. But don't let a man that isn't divine become one with you. Always be aware with what ingredients he will be pouring into you. Read him when he isn't watching. Study him when he isn't around. Know his ugly and his bad. There's a difference between the two. Decide if you can digest his insecurities. Decide if you can sympathize with his demons. And please, for the sake of you, accept love when it comes.

Words

Words for my daughter to tattoo on her body when the temptation comes...

.I am a star the sky couldn't hold. My walk is a parade of all the brave women that came before me. I am alive and I plan to stay that way. A temple, I am. And every bruise on my skin, a stained glassed window, they are. I am pure and I plan to live that way. To breathe that way. I have a womb built to house generations. There is an angel outlined in my shadow. There is a God that kisses me hello every morning. I am a woman. I am a girl who speaks queen and lives princess. I have a throne for a body. My scars may be ugly but my character looks nothing like them. I look nothing like them. The mirror always wears me well. I've been dealt bad cards but they were never good enough to take me out. I am still here. Covered in blood and prayer; everything that I am made of. I am still here and I am dancing. Tell them I am dancing in this imperfect body. I am still dancing with my flaws. I laugh with my insecurities. I kiss my tears when they come. I am deeply, insanely, unapologetically in love with myself. I love for myself. I love. This skin is my cape. I am more than flesh and bone. I am more than breasts and booty. Shake the world, I do. I am more. I am more. I am more.. I am enough.

Nappy-Headed

Mom says a woman's crown is her glory.
I remember how ugly my glory used to hurt me.
Whenever mom would
brush my hair she'd call it
the journey to a
woman's beauty.
She'd say
"women who are ugly don't know pain."
She'd say,
"this is
how you love the pain"
Mom erased the
kinks out of my naps.
I'd dig my nail into my
skin praying for a
bruise to outdo my
tender-headed behind.
Mom would scold me saying
"A woman's body is
her temple and
there's no need for
stained glass windows."

She'd tug my hair harder.

Mom knew how to paint beauty on a body.

Her lover taught her

How to bury a grave

into skin and

convince the world you're not rotten.

She'd tug harder.

He taught her how to turn bodies into battlefield,   to

walk like a soldier.

She'd tug harder.

He convinced her that his fists were only hearts from

cupid's arrows

That they were just the way he loved

She'd tug harder.

That this was just the way men loved.

She'd tug harder.

That this was love's texture.

Done.

I turned and looked at mommy's rugged skin.

She smiled revealing what's left of the teeth he hadn't loved yet.

Of the hair he hadn't tugged out yet.

He brushed the kinks out of my mother's body.

He loved the glory out of her crown.
And
The royal out of her palace.

Pops

If you look closely

    You may see my father more than I have in a lifetime.

        This is what a girl with daddy issues looks like.

            Black black skin.

            Dreadlocks.

            Big smile.

        A face I still can't recognize.

            My father...

            I'm afraid

Someone taught him how to leave a woman when she's late.

    Rolling Stones only leave behind the DNA.

        I have a crime scene of a face

        I've been told I have his nose.

            His mouth.

            His temper.

The Ghetto of Eden

I want to tell you this over the flowers,

the dinner,

the candle light

The moon

I'm afraid if I open my mouth too wide

you may recognize the screaming scars

You may see the burn victim he engraved in me.

Fact

I don't think a man can love my father out of me.

I believe my light at the

end of the tunnel is the

fire under a blunt.

I'm trying to out smoke his flame.

To leave him like he left me .

A man is supposed to teach his daughter how to love another one

To be loved back.

I don't know how to love you.

I want to tell you this.

I want to introduce you to my fire without burning you

Everything I touch melts, king

and I don't want to turn you to puddle with a crown on top.

I want you to stay despite

The tragedy

Of me.

I'm sorry about the fire in me.

It's a birth defect my father forgot to take with him

amongst the beautiful

memories he forgot

to leave behind for a

daughter to cherish.

I don't tell you these things.

Instead

I watch you talk about life and the beauty of it all.

Or

The ugly of it all.

Or the in between of it all.

I just take a sip of my drink

Praying it'll kiss the flame to death.

Wishing you could kiss me to life.

The beauty of it all.

The ugly of it all.

The fire it all leaves behind

Diary

I used to stand on balconies like this one.

Towering over all the

yellow

red

green

black.

The sea

of small bodies swaying back and forth.

I would stand here wanting to dive, into

all the busy people

after their lazy days....

It's that time of night where my neighbor cries.

I grab a bottle.

Sit and listen.

She can do something I can't.

Rain.

I wish I could be so full of tears

that they overflow and water my skin

like they do hers.

She's so alive.

I wish to be alive like that one day.

Nubia

A black woman is crying
And the world is silent-reverent.
For a black woman is watering herself.
She is being born again.
She is catering to.
She is taking care of.
She is handling business.
A black woman is crying.
Let her cry.
She knows what
she needs to do.
She always knows
How to water herself
When the sun is dead.

Once upon a little black girl, I wanted to find a boy with the whitest skin and the easiest hair and I wanted to fall in love with the boy. And I wanted to have his children. And I remember telling everyone I wanted to do this and my girlfriends would tell me they wanted this, too. So, we would buy the white Barbie with the long hair and we would imagine and we would have so much fun being everybody else on television and in the magazines because we were so ugly when we were ourselves.

We would play M.A.S.H and call these estranged white men our husbands. It wasn't because of the aesthetic or the blue in the eye or the straight of the hair. It was because of the protection of his looks. It was the camouflage in that skin. It was that sameness that would keep you alive. I think, for a moment there we, children, we, little girls, with our baby dolls, wedding planning and tea parties, were plotting ways to keep our babies safe while we were babies.

Barbie's Closet
I haven't been very good at love.
The last time I tried it was on a playground.
Avery didn't have anything to play with
so
I gave him my Barbie doll
It was embarrassing for him to hold her
so he ripped Barbie's head off to make
her look more masculine.
That's when I realized I loved him.
I vowed if we ever played trust fall
I would not catch him on purpose.
Love teaches you to keep your arms behind your back
when someone's falling for you
so the crash is damaging enough
to remember you by the scars
Paralyzing enough to stay by your side.
Bruise enough to pick at your ugly.
I remember being so confident
about love back then
there was no question.
The answer always sat in front of me with
Barbie's head buried in his dirty small palms

along with the prayer for masculinity.

Stay with me.

The day I became bad at love

the sun and the clouds were flirting.

The wind whispered love songs in my

ears and made my hair dance.

Isn't She Lovely tranced into every room in the house

and a smile

stumbled between everyone's lips.

Stevie's music blindly stumbles into any room

And puts a sun in the sky when there wasn't one.

On behalf of my family; I can say we all were happy.

But there came a crash.

always, remember there's a landing

you can't stay innocent when

he starts finding white stockings

frilly socks

school uniforms

And pigtails sexy

Dark skin.

Broad shoulders

My grandmother took him in.

her a heart was

a shelter.

He was a foster child

she was a fine tuned playground for the wounded.

I never teased him.

My skin was strictly a blanket for unwritten poetry.

I was the cover of a bible.

I had lips meant to kiss sippy cups

And pinky promises.

He told me to go into the closet and come out empty.

Wearing nothing but that black blanket of a skin.

He said it's a game that every little kid played.

That it was natural to feel this way

so it had to be far from a sin.

I went in the closet with Barbie in my palm next to my girlhood

they were drenched in the sweat only a man could muster.

I forgot to pick her up on my way out.

wearing what I wore

when I left my mothers womb.

Doesn't matter how many stages I get on

that day was the most vulnerable I ever felt

The most naked I've allowed on my skin

The most transparent I've ever been

Turning men into armies of conflict
pairs of arms that looked like graveyards
where love goes to die.
What do you tell the girls like me?
Who had love blown off of them like dust
You whisper off of your Bible when it's been too long and
the sins too heavy.
What do you tell the girls who grew to be scared of men
when they held
the most innocent parts of you
in the island of their hands.
The story buried herself in me
hiding in the walls of my mouth
calling him sick
while believing I was his sexual healing.
Still trying to find the cure for the remedy.
Love became as plastic as my Barbie doll
I forgot to pick up.
As fragile as my girlhood I left in that closet.
I'm now red handed from all the hearts I break
trying to protect mine.
Love is "it" in my hide and go seek and that closet is still
base

My ghost, she still lingers there.

I miss the lover in me.

The little girl

who if I saw you

with no toys to play with

I would give you my Barbie.

If I saw you with no love I would give you my heartbeat

didn't matter how dirty the palms,

or unholy the desires.

I've built another closet

Found a shirt with hearts on the sleeves

I look like a mascot for the love I don't carry

but still wish I did.

Bring me the day where I can love properly

with no strings attached

less puppet, more human.

the scars so beautiful

I give them names

so others won't realize I was ever broken.

Pinot

Whatever it is that keeps bringing you to this whiskey bottle
Is the same thing that keeps bringing you to that altar
Sunday mornings.
Whatever it is that's keeping you away from that Bible
Has not been keeping you.
You've been falling all the while.
This is how you've learned to run from God to god.
You don't stand still long enough to hear Him.
Say your prayers fast enough to get back to them.
Just as long as they've been said.
And I don't blame us.

Religiositonianism

Surely, there's a God.

And there, too, are many gods.

Pick your poison, child.

Cold War

2/14

           11:54p.m.

        roses are red

        violets are blue

        I wonder which color

the war has bruised you.

        it's been miles since

        i've felt you.

        your seed,

        he's walking now.

        he can take two steps.

        your wife,

        I'm crying often

        I don't know when I'm not.

        all I can think of is death.

        whether or not

it's met you yet.

If it has,

when it does,

if it does,

how will you

introduce you?

will you introduce

you?

or will you

introduce us?

tell it about

the son you

never met

the son who wears

your face better

than you do.

the wife who

wears

your t-shirts

looser than you.

the moon is

watching

us both.

watching your

side of the bed

still outlined with

the imprint of

your body.

I imagine

your gun pointed

to the sky

threatening

whatever god

there is

for keeping

us apart.

on such a day.

such a life.

roses are red

violets are blue

does the distance

bruise you?

too?

2/15
12:01

Down the Line   And this is why love is spectacular. Here you are, wandering the world with all of these thoughts and emotions that are both beautiful and ugly but you have no one to share your beauty with. You also have no one to share your ugly with. So there you are, wandering. Laughing, all the while. Crying, all the while. Dancing, all the while. Fighting, all the while. Drinking, all the while. Living, all the while. Then you meet someone who has your beauty and your ugly and "all the while" stops. The world ain't so lonely no more. You meet someone who also thought they were all alone. And you both have a little secret. You both take the masks off. You have been kissed before. You meet them. You've never been kissed before. You meet them and you always have a home to come to. The day can be as long as it wants. It can be as ugly as God designed it. Suddenly, you are a soldier with all the scars from the battles of your past lovers. They bandage you well. They bring you in. They forgive you again and again. They tell you that you are still beautiful with it all off. And that is why love is spectacular. It brings light to a room that already believed itself was shining, all the while.

"The Lord God said, "It is not good for the man to be alone. I will make a helper suitable for him." (Gen. 2:18)

Day 6

So God looked at Adam and got sad and creative. These are the best things to happen to any artist. His hands started twitching. He tucked His son in and took pieces of him and Him and made her and put her here. The garden didn't have any color until she yawned.

Shine, Sun, Shine

The day is tired.

let our moans be its lullaby.

labor with me, will you…

until the earth yawns

sending gusts of wind

through your hair

stretching it

like the arms of a

tiny child on a

Sunday morning.

a small miracle

the light that only a sunrise

can shine blending

with the kinks

the twirls

the curls

the bending

"Good morning"

your lips say

"Good mourning"

my body beckons

for this is how we

bury dead skin.

this is how we bury

ugly nights.

the bloody ones

we spent

with strangers.

oh, the empty bodies I slept in...

how cold they made me....

pour me a drink and

I'll pour into you.

for this has been war

a toast to the scars.

your mouth is home.

don't stop welcoming me.

Of Men & Mayhem

I know a man that carries magic and gospel in his pocket.
he runs his fingers through them often
they stick to him
so what he touches turns into that/them.
magic and gospel live on my spine, he has left him there
whenever my back needed having.
I know a man that has made every song true.
every note, wind that I hold onto the backs of when it
needs having
things that I once named heaven
fell to earth.
fell to regular.
with him, holidays are every tomorrow.
he has made a town out of my stomach.
there are ornaments hanging from my ribs
bells swinging from my cages
my heart draped in Christmas lights and red.
wine, a man and woman are drinking Jesus miracle.
Having romantic lunch in my gut.
They are discussing everything that knows nothing of them.
They are so small with a love so big, so fat, so unhealthy

you could sweat with it.

Look from the rooftops of my limbs at the world he's made out of my body.

The geography of my blood.

I am the city named after him

all is background to his silhouette.

He reflects shadow and grace.

Magic and gospel.

And we are dancing.

In a space where there is no rhythm

In a land we can only feel it.

His heart is my radio

And I never turn the station.

for the record never loses soul

Our feet never lose their sole

He and I.

We are the perfect space for love to get warm when it is cold.

I love him with all of me.

I love him with my dead skin.

I love him with my graying hairs and their stories.

I love him with all of me.

I love him all for me.

Flesh of flesh.

Limb for limb.

Teeth of teeth.

Blood for blood.

Bone of bone.

So violently, I love him

Cause this is what sacrifice is.

Violent.

Cause that is what love is.

Violent.

Making a canvas out of skin and bed sheets.

Because it's beautiful.

Because it hurts.

Because one can't be without the other.

Because...

the magic in his palm crucifies and resurrects me in one stroke.

The gospel on his tongue is the backbone of my breath.

He only brings them out for me.

He saves himself for me.

All hem for me.

All hymn for me.

The Ground Below

You can't tell the difference between the lover and the soldier.

They both walk with hope on their shoulders

&

a longer way from home due to it

&

They are in pain but they can't stop coming back.

The lover will plant their teeth in your skin asking for more.

The soldier will place their bullet in your skin asking for more.

More room.

More land.

More love.

More soil.

More freedom.

More captivity.

We return after, wiping the dust from our eyes,
looking at ourselves in the mirror for what feels like the first time.

We clean the skin and all below it.

We dwell a little longer on the scars

that love left.

Boy, do I war you.

Welcome

a sweet home, your love is.
        the flight was long.
        the hotels, rotten.
smelling of sweat and dry liquor on some strange man's tongue.
the flight was ever-ending and sleepless
    opening and closing my ears
    the traffic was stubborn, honey
    the luggage was heavy, sugar.
    but I'm home.
I've come home to God's fanciest dessert.
what a sweet home, you are.

Blackity

Ain't no black like my black.
Her bones brittle with kool aid and blood
a jungle juice that tastes like cool summer nights
the ones we believed ourselves to be invincible
with tomorrow as a promise rather than probably,
a drunk uncle electric slidin' on your poverty line,
grandma's mac and cheese, a heaven they forgot to write about,
mom's laugh so big, you can fit a party in it,
the moon sayin' wassup to the hood
there's a new body to pray about.
but ain't no black like my black.
my black ain't scared of your rooms
and your heartless government.
my black will creep into any corner.
my black, Assata.
my black, Baldwin.
my black, Martin.
my black, Malcolm.
my black is loud.
my black don't come off.
my black be permanent.

my black be something to celebrate about.

my black be a skin to cry on.

my black, a parade.

my black, a home.

my black, a skin.

my black, a cape.

my black, a shine.

my black, a gospel.

my black, a glory

my black, a soul.

my black, a jealous god.

my black. always.

The Fall of Man

When I love you forever becomes I lost you forever.

Found Lost

We are standing on opposite sides of the room just like the day we met. Except that day she didn't have tears in her eyes. Except that day I wasn't holding back mine. //Women cry freely// I reach my hand out as if her skin were closer. I want her to be closer. I want my arms to be home enough for her. My words to be contract enough for her. My tongue, a signature. My coming home, security. She says she is leaving. She says she needs a break. I want to stop her and promise her the moon like all the other nights. She carries my world out with her. I am left with empty, calloused hands. I am my father's son.

Eden

The garden stands still.

I don't think there's ever been a time where silence didn't make sense.

where my body felt more like sin.

A burden that I have not found an altar for.

We don't know if we are hiding from God or each other.

He doesn't believe like he used to, he says. I have never seen a man cry before today.

Adam is standing with his back to me

to protect me from The Creator.

His hands stretching to both sides of the forests

pleading in our name.

calling this place home.

I can still taste the sweet fragrance on my tongue.

we know nothing else.

Its soft smooth texture clumped between my teeth.

did you create us instead of mercy.

I know not what to do with my hands any more.

did we forget to give forgiveness a name

There has to be a safer me somewhere out there.

all we know is here.

if a prayer is said

with no one around to hear it

does it make a sound.

Adam's fingertips are coming back to him empty and filled with leaves and branches.

A plead is the last we gave to that wind.

Unsure of our bodies and what to do with them while in them.

When I listen closely, I'm sure I heard Him calling my name.

God is crying all the while.

Exodus

And so I stopped writing about you.

Then you appeared in my prayers,

And so I stopped talking to God.

Then you showed up on every face in front of me,

And so I stayed inside.

Then I saw your ghost in the smoke

And so I stopped smoking.

Then I dreamed about you.

You were good there.

You still loved me there.

You still found me necessary.

You took me and placed me in all of your voids.

And so I stayed there.

And so I could never wake up.

I never wanted to.

And this is why love is so unhealthy.

It makes you want to be alive in a very limited capacity.

And freedom isn't so fun anymore.

I'm afraid that I'll never be able to love anyone like I did you.

That even if tried, my body would tell me over and over,

"this isn't home."
And I'll spend eternity trying to convince body that this is.
That we're warm enough here.
That the people are nice here.
Although we both know
we are deserving of more than an okay love.
An enough love.
We are supposed to be filled to the brim with love
that it spills onto everything we touch.
So I have left you in places you have never been.

My bed is always full of you.
My ring finger is always empty of you.

The Fall

And I don't know where a love goes when its lost its home.
I do know that these nights are endless
much like the ride back to my place
after an evening of mistakes
and gin.
I think the love goes looking for us in places we may have
left it.
But, I can't hear myself over the music
the DJ's got Fetty Wap going
and this is everyone's song
so everybody's throwing their body into other bodies.
Fingers pointing to a godless sky,
someone spills their drink in my drink,
which is awkward,
and the only words I could make out of the slurred voices
were
"I want you,
be mine,
again".
And I know I'm sinking to a new low
when the basic song begins to mean something.

The Ghetto of Eden

In the same places I go to forget you.
Right here, in the lyrics of a sweaty party.
much like where we met.
Only then we hadn't felt each others skin.
Only then, we hadn't made the promise to not sound like
our parents.
Standing on opposites sides of a room
cleaner than our relationship.
A mouth full of tears, wine and truth,
I tell you I'm sorry I always make a mess of my mess
and I can't find a place to put myself most times.
You claim your arms are home enough.
I look at them strong and heavy but shaking as if you didn't
mean
to let those words go.
There's not much left in you to love me the way you never
knew how.
I tell you give me time.
I'll find self control in the wind outside.
You'd joke that I was cheating on you with my mind.
Smile, knowing there's nothing funny about
not sleeping at night.
And we're at the good part of the fight..

where all bets are off.

We don't know if we are looking at each other

or for each other

but we are enjoying the yelling,

the bruising of a something once innocent and pure.

Tears blurring the image of a lover we will have to soon forget.

Telling the truth about what hurt when the love was happening

and not caring how bad the words feel

when we let them go

as long as they're said.

I'm ready to leave like

always

had an easier time opening the door to let myself out than

let people in.

But you,

you are more patriotic about us.

Hand placed over chest,

mouth preaching the dedication of those cold nights, warm days, gripping moments

that made us stay despite the scars we could never heal

you have invested in this love.

The Ghetto of Eden

You've realized how naked I left you
when it was all over.
And the night is still endless.
The party just starting
and I can't think of a better home than you
when these gatherings become too close for skin
my mind too clogged to hear.
I think of who I was when I was with you,
how I miss her most.
The laugh you placed on her tongue still lingers somewhere
in the wind
wishing for you to say something to bring her back.
I don't know which one of us was more difficult to hold
onto
But when a Fetty Wap song comes on in a party that you're
in…
When the words are spilling out of drunken lips
and you are five shots in trying to forget me,
do you think of me?
Do I still fit in the small moments?
Am I still in the detail of things,
weaving together all the fabric.
Doing the work of loving you

better than most have.

I believe the hardest part of it all

was trying to hold onto another body

and my own

without running out of breath.

Of Mayhem and Men

                I loved once
                Can't you tell…
       There is a part of me you don't see.
      There is a part of me that was once here.
There is a me that is a mad woman in another city
she is now running wild on the backs of some wind.
    Riding through the quietest neighborhoods,
          bleeding a dead city red,

  begging the people to come out and play with her.
  She has tears in her eyes but a smile on her face,
           Cuervo on the tongue
  She knows not what to do with her hands anymore.
  She knows they belong somewhere inside of yours.
        Attached to your waist perhaps
on your cheeks to keep them warm

            when the world is cold.
           She is still loving you
     She has not accepted that you have left
             and I stayed.

I'm still loving you somewhere.

I am still trying to learn

what my body is here

for if it is not to be against yours.

In another city,

the people are saying your name.

For she wanders

the streets throwing it

on the top of her lungs

for everyone to see.

They wonder what

beautiful name could

have loved such a

mad untamed woman...

She is running through their streets

asking everyone to come outside

and play with her.

The air is cool,

she doesn't bite.

She's just hoping you could hear her too,

I miss that part of me.

I pray for her sanity often
But if God were listening,
she wouldn't be there
she would be here with me
and
You would still be loving me.

Say it From the Rib

My husband is a drunk. He don't love me like he love that bottle. He love that bottle like he used to love me. His fingers wrapping around it's waist. Drinking from it like it's holy water or somethin'. I don't know what's in him he wanna kill. He found somethin' in him, he don't like and he tries to get rid of it everyday. The answer ain't at the bottom of that bottle, baby. It's sayin' no at the top. But he don't wanna hear that. He wanna hear himself. All hours of the night turning the walls of our house into punching bags. I'm afraid they won't be enough one day. His fists will crave my skin in ways they never have before. I'm more afraid that I forgot his touch so much that I'll be okay with that. Any love he gives is welcomed as long as it's a love. And maybe I need a drink, too.

The Chorus

I am in love with a hymn.

the song in his voice.

the fountain behind his lips that I drink

from on mornings when I feel like drowning.

I find myself running his name over my tongue

like a comb does an afro.

He untangles me.

My brain is trying to hold on to him.

It knows what time does to beautiful things.

We found each other like broken people do

you made my wounds feel pretty and I healed yours too.

tell me,

what wind is this

that has gathered in my bones

whispering secrets of life through them.

what flesh is this

that when I showed you my flaws

and asked you to bare with me

you placed your naked on my skin

and wore my body for clothing.

what song is this

that my heartbeat has become a drum solo.

what home is this

that all the people before you

were cigarette scented hotel rooms.

rotten bed sheets and

something to gossip

about in the morning

I used to think love was like

a church building

a place for everyone but me

but you were gospel enough to bring

me to my knees at your altar.

what sermon are you

that you made me pray again

the journey to you was godless.

but praise God for the palms

yours being the sweatiest

river my hearts ever swam in

your arms,

the sweetest home

I've ever known.

please, don't stop

welcoming me.

For doesn't love

last till infinity twice in one lifetime.

ii.

It's one of those nights again.

You have gone

in your eyes.

I have tears in mine.

They are trying to create a

river

streaming

down my cheek

serene enough to

convince you to stay a bit longer

even if it means to watch me rain.

We apologized for

everything except ourselves.

We love God too much to say sorry for existing.

So you turn to leave your back,

blemish in the horizon.

your skin,

a raisin in the sun.

And from here, you look

like

my father.

You have chosen the

world over me

Is this the meaning of it all?

A dare.

to fall and name my

bruises after you

find the rhythm in your

heartbeat and make a

song out of it.

to bleed so much into

someone that when

you see them

you see yourself.

Sometimes we made love

like tomorrow wasn't coming too.

Other days, I try to forget

I loved at all.

Every night,

I wonder of all the lips

you kissed after mine.

Did you ever wonder of me?

Did your palms ever miss my palms?

your chest ever miss my cheek?

Your shoulders,

my lips.

Your neck,

my breath.

if your anatomy

missed me at all

did it trust you

enough to tell you?

seeing that you were the one that

gave its heart away

and forgot to ask for it back.

I'm so red handed from

the heart you left

that when we pulled

apart it looks like

I've just been crucified.

and I've been mourning

my death ever since.

iii.

and isn't this love

we are old now.

closer to our graves

than we have ever been

and we have

God to thank for that.

for this.

whatever this

has been for

the last fifty years of trying.

I am fingertips away from you.

I am trying to hold onto time

and whatever I can remember of us.

I say,

the day will come when

we will crumble to dust.

where we will close

the last chapter of the book.

we will go wherever life goes

when it is all over.

and we will go rejoicing.

on evenings like this.

I draw the sky on your chest

to prepare your body for

it's new home.

we are light years

away from young

and I can still smell the

rum of a drunken

20-year-old boy

on your tongue.

you still smell

like your worst sin

and I find myself

loving that part

of you the most.

When this world is too burden to live

I call on the nights we spent seventy-five years young

drunk pillow-talking about heaven

I promise if I reach it first

I am prepared to paint your face on

the pavement to make sure

the streets are really made of gold.

and wait next to God for your arrival.

The God that we prayed to

in the midst of the arguing.

The God that kept us together

when the storms came.

I'll wait right next to Him

for when you come.

with a choir of angels singing behind us.

if love were a texture it would be your skin

if love could speak, it would say your name

you are my favorite hymn.

to sing.

For Spike

        you choose the gentler words
        when the room clears
        and the dust settles.
you remind me I have a lot more woman to become.
        I have more black to unfold.
        more room to unlearn the learned.
there's always more fight in the spine.
more back in the bone.
you are all that and ever.

Ezekiel

slip through the fingers.
                be water.
                be wind.
          be carried and carry.
so when the storm comes you can
              dance with it.
           when it leaves,
       you can breeze after it.
this world chews away at the skin somedays
      but we are not the world.
we were made on a different day, we are kind.
            we are loving.
              still dancing.
                still wind.
          still a home for glory.
                 still.

Requiem

so I've been around the sun about 21 times now and I learned a few things about this body & skin. it was told to me at a very young age that my body was somebody's temple. that it absolutely wasn't mine. it belonged to an angry white-bearded man in the clouds who swore that I was his but we never really got around to talking about it & he's shy & so he never comes around or talks back. I learned who to not put in it, what not to put on it, how to heal it, how to scar it. in similar days, the television gave me reason to hide it more. my body wore me more than I wore her. she pretended to be cold when it was hot. she was so heavy and I recall being strictly embarrassed to be breathing in her. I separated myself from my body, mentally, as an escape. I always imagined myself in some other girl's skin. wearing way more beauty and being good at being it. with much less to carry. much less to cover up. much less to learn to love. coupled with this sentiment was my desire for a new skin. I think there was once a time, & so many black girls can probably relate to this, where there were so many complaints we just had in our living. first, we were girls & we were always preparing to turn into women. we were so worried about our bodies. if we weren't tucking tissues in our bra, drenching our face in makeup or shaving super early and soon, this insecurity became more. it became the total hatred of my body's existence here. the other kids would tell me how my skin was too dark, too full of flaw. my body was taking up too much space. I decided to find ways to lose my existence in this body. I made fun of other people so everyone wouldn't look at me too long. this soon translated to a fear of being alone w/ myself. I wanted to hurt my body. I wanted to leave it behind. very far behind. it's in this dance with suicide that possibility rings the most. what can I do with tomorrow? I can always choose not to show to it. I can always decline its invitation. depression is a very dark place with terrible games of possibility and chance it's in this possibility of living that I am learning to find an overwhelming love and desire to live in this thing every single day that I am blessed to. the mornings are much easier to see and I believe that much of it is attributed to this year. 2015 was full of ups and downs that often felt too much to handle. too heavy to carry. & it was all so tiring. there were days where there was a new fulfillment of a tragic possibility that I never wanted to see come true. & there were days that were a running water of joy. & in those days I was endless. it was in this land of beautiful mess that I learned to play the game of possibility & to play on the team of living. for the celebration of seeing through. demanding the day & fighting for the arrival of it. when shit hits the fan, I celebrate for the possibility of a glory soon to come. I'll tell you now, the battle scars are ugly and painful but sometimes pain is the medicine. breath is the victory. prayer is the healing. It is possible that a very ugly thing will happen tomorrow. it is more possible that you will make it beautiful. for you must believe in tomorrows, too. you were made to see them. they were made just to see you. you have to be there. this is not something to merely say. this is something to spread with the touch and the hug and the breath. this is something to live and only you can question what this means: to live words. what is it to give yourself and sacrifice to words. to make the Bible a

Tuesday. make the Qur'an a forgiving moment. you must decide that tomorrow is a sight to see. you must decide that loving yourself is just as attainable as touching your own skin. hold your breath & use it for good.

Leftover Bones to Pick

I am learning how to keep my secrets in my mouth more.

but there are times where I don't want to.

I'm afraid I'll die with all of these secrets.

my family will mourn me

never knowing who it is they are really mourning.

for all of me died with me.

Space

You come to the altar three times in your life.

The first is to give your sins to God.

Because your demons are taking up too much space.

The second is to kiss your partner.

Because your love is taking up too much space.

The third is to die.

Because heaven needs you to take up some space.

God is present every single time.

Healing

There's a gospel inside you.

Open your mouth and preach that song.

yeah, yeah.

Preach that song.

yeah, yeah.

Let everyone year you.

yeah, yeah,

Let everyone hear you.

You don't need no church building.

no, no.

All you need is in that tongue.

All you need is spine.

bone.

blood.

water.

melanin.

yes, yes.

Melanin, that's a psalm too.

Look at your skin.

Look at that thing.

Look at that big beautiful sky.

A river flows below it.

Carrying every woman that stayed alive with you in mind.

yes.

All war is about it.

yes.

That skin in your hands.

your hands...

Run yo' fingers over that skin.

Wrinkled or straight.

Loose or strict.

Run those fingers over that skin.

yeah, yeah

Don't skip the bruises.

no, no.

Sing the bruises.

The melodic notes, they are. Written by Yahweh Himself.

They say choose the lesser of two evils but I never wanna choose evil.

I never wanna eat the apple.

The Dance

we must ask ourselves...
        when will the day come
    when the black man can come to the table
          for a slice of pie,
            put his feet up,
          unbuckle his belt,
       open his calloused hands
        and say his prayer
      without being killed for
   being born in threat and blood.
        breathing too loud
         eating too eagerly
          making a mess
         in that damn skin.
      without being killed
    before his prayer can end.

being black is like a party. it's lit. there's music, people, drinks and joy. but, man, it is hot in there. we are dying out here.

The Ghetto of Eden

the room is sweatin'. the niggas are leanin. over jokers and tens. laughter and talks of bitches and money. green passed through middle fingers and forefathers. missin from home. we are brown to every bone. in that bitch is crazy. and everything that won't understand me. and you think mirrors are sometimes hard to look inside. her legs are wheelchairs. so I'm between them. to heal, too. night stands are covered in gin. darker than this skin. it's scary to live in cause. we are bound to die in. justice is hungry. so this room I stay in. there, I know they out here, hunt. in. coming. three houses down they moved the niggas out. the better ones in. look out. side of the story matters. over mind. nigga, you see the signs. that say hide your skin to stay in alive in it. sold my life for rims and tens and windows that were tinted. cause we ain't just men. ain't safe in too much melanin. costs more than breath. please come before my death. but tonight the room is sweatin. the niggas are leanin' over jokers and tens. laughin louder than the voices. they wanna silence.

Be Knowin'

Behind every "party girl" is
a man she'd never leave her room for.
I miss being an excuse with you.
A reason to stay indoors and seek each other's minds
for either a story or a laugh.
You're a tear stain now.
You're annoying to bring up to my friends
and myself.
You've made me cry enough to drown out the reason
and yet it still floats
on the bayou of my tongue,
our love comes up for air
once in a while
searching for us to breathe, again.

Barbie's Closet Reminisce

We women know how to bleed until we are wine.
Fermented eve jungle juice.
swaying in glass.
We don't talk about the man that happened last night.
We talk about the nigga that happens every morning
whose body won't stay buried.
Under our nails.
We draw red lines in backs.
A new slave master for the man whose black
won't get off my skin.
He comes home in the evening with a party stuck between
his teeth
and gunpowder on the tongue.
But, we women know how to bleed until we are wine
so I try not to sing too much of hem tonight.
No, tonight, we ain't worryin' about no broken man.
With that limp and that half smile.
And those heavy shoulders
that I would lean over in search of breath.
love ain't ever been healthy,
it killed Jesus Himself.

If it's done right,
it'll suck the air
out of any room
you're in.

Fill

it's a wonder, isn't it? How one can have so many friends and not have any friends. How one can have so many lovers and still have no lover. how one can have so much family and still no blood. How one can be so full and still be starving.

stay alive and be gentle with yourself. everyone was made in the image of Yahwah. everyone. we have the audacity to create despite all the adversity that says not to. you win everyday you wake up. you win in the moments you invest in a dream that receives laughter when it's told. but those voices aren't worth the sound. don't listen to them. go to that place. go to that very dangerous and honest neighborhood in your bones and do with them as you will. feel them and free them. take care of your mind. take care of yourself. pour into whatever you do but regroup and bandage yourself to continue on this journey of living. keep living. this world needs your song for as long as you are willing to sing it. this world needs your breath as long as you are willing to breathe it. this world needs your words as long as you are willing to say them. this world is you.

Something Happened to Outside

Outside ain't loud no more.

Outside ain't sweatin' no more.

The boys ain't throwin' the football.

The girls ain't jumpin' the rope.

Nobody lookin' at the streetlights for time.

Nobody lovin' the sun.

Nobody watchin' the moon.

Nobody talkin' to God.

Does it scare you that no one has a reason to look to the sky anymore?

What war did this?

What trigger was pulled?

In whose hands?

Who that movin' in down the block?

They got blue eyes that only see green.

We got brown eyes that still ain't seen sky.

Still ain't see

Who's free?

Whose seat is still empty at the dinner table?

Who took that black boy?

Who told him that tears are women.

who told him that fists were men, who is still trying to
outrun their skin, who died that we forgot to mourn, whose
blood is still on that sidewalk, who, who, who is the new
body to bury, to burn, to black, to blue, to earth, to heaven,
to glory, to Him, to sorry, to that world back there don't
love what you love, nah, they don't like us breathing this
breath.
Mom says they killin' us.
I asked who.
She said all of us.
I asked who doin' the killin'.
She said everybody, baby.
Everybody.
And everybody went on home.
Afraid to be six feet deep in that dirt we used to
fill our hands with when we were children,
when we found mess funny.

Untitled

Ain't no black like my black.
Ain't no skin like my skin.
Ain't no love like my love.
I thank God for this reason to write.
This canvas to begin with. I take off the top of the pen And I place the rest of me in the sea. I tell the sun to follow me on home after. Let's rest after the day. Cause this freedom was worth it. It's always worth it.

Toy Soldier

    they haven't found a way to tax the wind yet.
    to put a "white only" sign above the water.
    to convince the sun to fall for another skin.
    the day's longer than lives.
yesterday, a black boy's body forgot how to keep breathing
    under the weight of your hand.
    this morning, his wife is learning her bed again.
    the space over there is the outline of a bible.
tomorrow, we're supposed to put our feet to the pavement
    and tell the world something.
    they call it a riot.
    I call it yawning.
    I call it singing this blood a new song.
    yes, one more like a lullaby.
    a hummed tune.
    while reading the eulogy again and again.

The Rain

I woke up this morning and something said pour.
so I slipped into my slippers
and ran to the window
fogging it with the sky in my breath
waiting for the rain to come.
I waited and waited.
when rain comes, it always brings a poem with it.
the rain never came, so the poem never did.
I went to sleep that night
something said pour.
this time I didn't run to the window.
this time I ran to myself.
drenching the notebook with the rain in my tears.
and tomorrow is today.
tomorrow is today.
be impatient and wait for yourself.

Kodesh

You don't come around friends like you often.
the ones who have given you good days and saved you after the bad ones.
the ones who can pray with you and for you again after.
eighth grade I didn't take my smile seriously
would wear it for camouflage
this is what it feels like to live in a jungle.
to treat everyday like it's a war to survive and not one to live.
You sat next to me and haven't left yet.
The bell rings in all of my mistakes and you still find reason to stay
on every today, I thank whatever drew you on my canvas
before the mourning.
buried you deeper under my skin than blood.
I haven't been alone since
and if you aren't proof that love is the thickest air,
I mean, it is just fat and overflowing everything, taking up space.
and you never made me feel in the way.
I hear,
when you are blessed with something heavy,

you shed it everywhere.
I have left you in cities that don't know your name.
calling you
a warm kinda love.
a home for the homeless like me.
with no roof to call me safe.
they call you
a take your shoes off kinda love.
a get comfortable in this kinda love.
a there's not a tomorrow I don't wanna see you laugh in kinda love.
my best friends taught me how to walk again
how to put one drunken foot in front of the other
after the day just left you hung over and dry and tired and alone.
to leave the house while the sun is still up
even though your heart is the color of night.
with a world refusing to dance under it.
this, right here, is what it means to have
best friends that are best friends with God.
when He's in the detail of the fabric.
right there
sewed to the wind.

in this moment you realize that you have a life worth living.

a song worth singing.

and the right voices that will always be worth listening to.

My father has left for the third time and I've been trying not to dance with the metaphors of that reality.

He has made it difficult to stand still again.
my body is trying to find him.
it's having a hard time believing that he is not above this earth anymore.
that I cannot feed him the anger that I've been trying to keep the world safe from.
I have not figured out what to do with myself without him here, that I've always been used to understanding that he was miles away but our love was always a conversation away.
a decision to be present away.
a forgiveness away.
and I tried.
believe me, I've tried.
I've tried to tell these nights that I could sleep through them.
I've tried to find you in other men.
I've looked for you at the bottom of bottles.
I've been looking for you for years.
why has death placed you back in my vision?
why did we have to reunite here?
In these dark back rooms

away from the noise.
The back of my hand pressed against my eyes
tears running of makeup I'd have to reapply
to keep the public from knowing,
giving me credit for the strength I don't have.
you've been living in my head but at least I could hear your voice.
now, you are permanently residing in my mind.
you're still the only man that can make me cry.
you are still my only love.
you are still my first love.
if you were breathing, I know you would find that funny &
be proud that something in this life went your way
you'd say you knew it.
you'd say I'm still your little girl.
you'd tell me to let you in.
I'd tell you I can't do that with you so far away.
so unable to parent.
so unwilling to be here.
I couldn't metaphorically let you in anymore.
I was greedy with my dreams of having a father.
I'd tell you that you don't deserve a daughter like me.

I never knew if this were me apologizing for all I've
become or all that I didn't.
what with me and your God's relationship being so at odds.
and I'd tell you that I wish I were all the other girls.
who made this womanhood look so easy.
who were annoyed by their father's presence.
who had the pictures.
of them.
together.
I cannot find that one of me and you.
before you left the second time.
the sun was on our back
and Sabbath on her way.
and I was so in love with you then.
and I screamed about it.
with closed fist.
knuckles to dry the stream
sputtering down my cheek.
and I can't find her anywhere.
I've been looking for us, dad.
I know you died searching, too.
a week before you left for the final time, you asked what
happened to us.

I'm good at a lot of things
that you've never seen me do.
but I have not been good at finding anything worth filling
your void.
you called it running.
I called it searching.
you called it pushing.
I called it reaching.
I'm sorry our verbs never agreed.
I'm tired, too, dad.
and I don't have any of the answers.
just a long, long prayer overwhelmed with wonders.
and maybes.
and ifs.
and anger.
and more anger.
and more I miss yous.
and hating admitting that.
and wondering if it's possible to do so when I can't
remember the last time you stood still long enough for me
to love you as properly as I know I can.
but until the next sunrise,
I have Marvin Gaye.

I have Take 6.

I have Ben Tankard.

embedded in the notes is your song, your baritone, I can hear you.

So that's where you went.

I don't blame you.

I can hear you in all the sunsets.

the beginning of every Shabbat.

you've become my Friday evenings.

I mourned you while you were still breathing.

I must tell you, despite what you may have left believing,

my love for you is in heaven.

I placed it there for safe keeping.

I hope we find it together

On that good day.

P.S.

It will always be a little colder without you here.

Generations

When I tell you that I was raised by a village of brown
women
this means I woke up to their laughter
it was the sound of the sun rising.
I mean I huddled silently outside the door when they cried.
I mimicked the gossip,
they'd swing their hips from side to side
lingering over the hot stove
in a sweaty kitchen and they ain't care.
they just wanted to feed you.
with bodies more useful than bed and bread.
aunt Velecia's laugh rises from her chest to the tip of her
full lips,
it falls like a song and reaches every corner of the room.
she wears her story in her high heels so she glides in her
throne.
cousin Christine wears the sass in her neck, the reason in
her shy smile.
she is in all of my favorite days.
her smile has taught me how to love my family.
Aunt Terri is

always a joke away from intimidating any harm back into the corner it came from.

any moment that I am fun, I am her.

my cousin Rhonda is still 20. she still dances like all black girls did. in their living room. in front of the TV, carefree about their faces missing from it.

I wanted to be a comedian when I was younger because you made me believe it was possible to be goofy and woman in the same body.

my god mommy April is the soul I still pray I can be a morsel of.

she outshines the sun and ain't never apologize for the chocolate on her skin.

& my mother.

when I'm myself, I'm her.

my mother is a glory and a victory.

she carries a world in her that doesn't fear any room she enters. I'm sure He made her smile the blueprint for yours.

I know tired days very well. This weight gives itself as a burden, like my worries have become another body I have to travel with. When these days happen, don't relish over the blessings given. Those aren't always permanent. Don't bask in the love of my lover as if it has become an only energy source, an only reason. My lover can always find their way out just as they entered. No, when these days come don't find solace in the future of when the sweat pays off. The work will bring glory. Don't put faith in the future victory. Imagine the beginning. The reason for you. The reason we are all here is much greater than the impermanence of here and all it brings. We have to figure that these days are full of something a bit more. This love has to mean something a bit more. We have to fill this breath with something more important. More crucial. More graceful. More mercy. When the tired days come, when I don't feel completely mine anymore, when I've wandered too far from the path...I imagine the beginning. You came in this world with one helluva task that the enemy is running breathless trying to take you out. Lean in. There's more bite in those bones.

The Garden

In the Garden lies the things we left behind on the way out. In the Garden lies everything we named with our own tongues rather than the things that were named for our tongues. In the river, there's a peace that keeps the seas flowing and rushing. The air is light and empty waiting for our breaths to fill it again. Women sing and dance with children on their hips, their eyes full of the child baring white that can only be found on the teeth of a smile. It's here you can take off the day, hang it in the closet and lay the burdens down. If I listen closely, I can hear the garden calling, waiting for us to claim the things that were our own again. Take back the joy stolen. Come relentless in blood and bone and a shout. Say this love is mine. Say this is music is mine. Say this gift is mine. Say this love is mine. This God is mine. No longer told what language to speak. What way to kiss. What body to wear. What worship to give. My skin is unconventional so I was born in the blood of other and I bask in this world's difficulty in naming me. Taming me. I was born with a name taken before given. I'll return to the garden, the home of my safety. And I'll give myself a new name this time. A name that holds the skin together. One that is difficult to say but proud to mean. Be loud with laugh. Make the giving of love the only option, again. Return to the garden. Plant the seed. Hold your body to the Light. Water yourself. And when the serpent comes, for he always does, feed him the apple.

Closing Prayer

And the people will continue living
And the moves will keep moving
And dance will keep dancing
Laugh will keep laughing
Praise will keep praising
Black will keep blacking
Black will keep blacking
Black will keep blacking
Hate will keep hating
Love will keep loving
Mourn will keep mourning
Until another day comes
A lovely other day
this day will bring Abba with it
this day will bring Gabriel with it
this day will bring Christ with it.
this day will bring trumpets with it.
this day will bring clouds with it.
this day will bring glory with it.
this day will bring a new garden.
and we can all lay down the weapons.
we can all go home rejoicing.

we can all go on singing.
we can bury the burden.
reuniting with the buried.
all forgiven.
all forgiven.
all forgiven.
all forgiven.
Ase.
Amen.

Jasmin Oya is a young writer and teaching artist from the city of Philadelphia and currently attends Oakwood University in Huntsville, Alabama as a Junior English Major. She is both a lover and a fighter who believes in the freedom and wellness of all people. Jasmin is dedicated to giving back to her community through her writing and living.

Twitter: @BlackJasminTea

Made in the USA
Lexington, KY
28 March 2016